3-D THRILLERS!

W9-BNS-351

BUGS

and the World's Creepiest Microbugs

PAUL HARRISON

New York • Toronto • London • Auckland
Sydney • Mexico City • New Delhi • Hong Kong

WHAT IS A

Bugs, creepy-crawlies, or mini-beasts—whatever you call them—are the mini-marvels of the animal world. Around 75 percent of all animals on the planet are insects.

Bugs galore

Almost all bugs come from a group of animals called arthropods. This is a large category that includes insects, which are animals with three body parts and six legs. Beetles, ants, and wasps are all insects. Arthropods also include arachnids, which are animals with eight legs, like spiders.

Wood lovers ▶

Wood lice are bugs that usually live in dark, damp places. They feed on decaying leaves and plants. Their tough, plated bodies protect them from predators.

Survivors ▶

Bugs are the great survivors of the animal kingdom—they were crawling around 200 million years before the dinosaurs arrived. These tough critters can handle extreme heat or cold, and the toughest of all is the cockroach—it can even survive without its head for up to a week!

BUG?

▲ **Slow movers**

The word *bug* includes another group of creatures, called gastropods. Slugs and snails belong to this group. Slugs and snails have a single large, flat foot that they use to push themselves forward, which puts them firmly in the creepy-crawly class!

TOUCH, TASTE,

Just like people, bugs can hear, see, taste, smell, and feel. But bugs are very different from us, so they experience all these senses in a different way, too.

▼ Eye see

Some bugs have enormous eyes! They're called compound eyes because they are made up of lots of little hexagons, or six-sided shapes. Each hexagon sees something slightly different, and the bug's brain puts the image together like a puzzle. The bigger a bug's eyes, the better the bug can see. Dragonflies have gigantic eyes, so they have amazing sight.

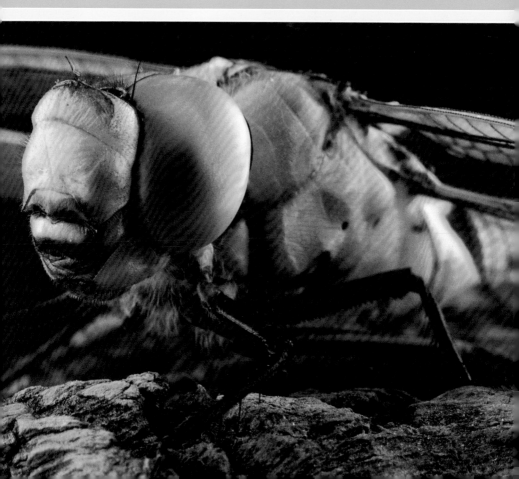

SEE, HEAR

◀ Good vibrations

Bugs don't have ears as we know them. Instead, they have fine hairs on their bodies that pick up the tiny vibrations made by sound. Crickets, however, do have something similar to ears: They pick up sounds through small holes in their forelegs.

The EMPEROR MOTH is a supersniffer. It can smell other moths up to 7 miles (11 km) away!

Sweet feet ▶

Some bugs use their mouths to taste food, but many flies and butterflies use their feet! A butterfly's feet can sense the sugar in nectar—the sweet liquid made by plants to attract insects—so the butterfly knows if something is good to eat or not!

ON THE MOVE

Bugs that live in different environments have developed different ways of getting around. The dragonfly is an expert in the air, the slug is a slow slider on the ground, and ants scurry up and down at a fast pace. A bug's life is suited to its method of movement.

▼ Lots of legs

Insects have 6 legs, spiders have 8, but most centipedes and millipedes have between 30 and 400 legs. One species of giant millipede can have up to 750 legs! Their short legs help them burrow underground very quickly when they need to escape predators.

◄ Hop to it!

The flea is king of the jumping world. It can jump over 100 times its own height—that's like a man jumping over the Washington Monument! In this way, fleas can hop onto a host, such as a cat; hitch a ride; and enjoy a meal!

WATER STRIDERS can skate on water—without sinking!

Slowpokes ▶
They may be slow, but snails can climb trees, slide across ceilings, and cling to almost anything. The sticky slime they produce helps them stick fast to surfaces.

LET'S PLAY . . .

Like all other animals, bugs spend most of their time either looking for something to eat or trying to avoid being eaten! Some bugs go to amazing lengths to make sure they're still around at the end of the day!

CATERPILLARS are eating machines! Some munch their way to 27,000 times their birth size.

Dinner? ▶

The best way to make sure you don't get eaten is to look like something that no one wants to eat. The giant swallowtail caterpillar wins the gross meal competition. When it is newly hatched, it has brown and white markings that make it look like bird droppings!

HIDE-AND-SEEK

◀ Eensy-weensy spider

The crafty crab spider doesn't bother building a web to catch prey. This sneaky predator lies inside flowers, waiting for its victims. It doesn't just hide, though. The crab spider can change color to match the flower it's hiding in. Not all bugs have good eyesight, so many end up as lunch for this patient spider.

Now you see it . . . ▶

Butterflies, moths, and caterpillars are masters of disguise. When the dead-leaf butterfly folds its brightly colored wings together, only the dull undersides of the wings (which are the color of a dead leaf) are visible. The wings are even leaf shaped, too.

SAFETY IN

Many bugs live in huge colonies. There are lots of advantages to living in a large group—there are more bugs to look for food, to protect the home from attack, and to care for young bugs and eggs.

High-rise home ▼

Few bug homes come bigger than soil-dwelling termites' mounds! A mound can be up to 20 feet (6 m) tall and is built over the termites' nest, which is buried underground. Termites build their mounds from dry mud to protect the nests below and keep them cool.

▼ Ordered society

Bugs that live in big groups are very well organized, with each bug having a role. In a beehive, the top bee is the queen, and she lays all the eggs. Another group of bees, called drones, mates with the queen. The worker bees find nectar to feed the hive and make honey. If the hive is attacked, it's their job to protect it, too.

NUMBERS

◀ Messing around on the water

The last place you would expect to find ants is on a river! When fire ants are flooded out of their home, they don't mind grouping together in a big cluster and floating down the river. They'll drift until they land somewhere dry where they can make a new home.

Deadly swarm ▶

Locusts are large plant-eating insects that normally live alone. However, when a few locusts get together, they can give off signals that attract more and more locusts, until billions of them appear and form a swarm. When a huge swarm gets hungry, it can strip fields bare for miles around.

GOOD BUG,

Bugs may be small, but they're important. They pollinate plants and flowers, helping them reproduce. Bugs are also Mother Nature's garbage disposals. They get rid of dead plants, dead animals, and even animal droppings! How? By eating them!

▼ Dirty job

One of the most important insects on the planet has one of the most unpleasant jobs. The dung beetle lives on waste from other animals. By eating this dung and then producing its own waste, this beetle helps put nutrients back into the soil. It also buries dung that holds seeds from plants and trees. Some of those seeds grow into new plants. Clever beetle!

BAD BUG

◀ Grub's up!

Some bugs eat other bugs, which is good news for gardeners! A gardener's best friend is the ladybug, because in its lifetime a single ladybug can eat up to 5,000 plant-loving pests. That's one hungry lady!

Public enemy ▶

In many parts of the world, people suffer from mosquito bites. The female mosquito uses her long, sharp mouthparts to pierce the skin of an animal or human and drink the victim's blood. Some mosquitoes pass on a disease called malaria, which can be fatal for people.

◀ Cleanup

Ever wonder why you don't see many dead birds or dead wild animals? That's because dead creatures are a great source of food for beetles and maggots (which are baby flies). They can eat up a bird in just a few days!

LITTLE AND

Bugs come in all shapes and sizes—they can be so small you need a microscope to see them. Or they can be big enough to give you a scare if you weren't expecting to see one!

▲ Itty-bitty insect

Meet the fairyfly—possibly the smallest insect on the planet! The tiniest fairyflies are less than a quarter of a millimeter in length, which makes them impossible to see. They are minuscule wasps that lay their eggs on the eggs of other insects, so that their babies have an instant meal when they hatch.

◄ Snail alert

The giant African land snail is the largest snail on Earth. This enormous gastropod can grow up to 15.5 inches (39 cm) long and can weigh as much as 2 pounds (907 g).

LARGE

Big is beautiful ▶

As well as being some of the most beautiful insects around, dragonflies and damselflies are also some of the biggest. Their wingspans can measure up to 7.5 inches (19 cm) in length.

▼ Meet Goliath

Beetles make up a quarter of all living animals on Earth! The most impressive of all beetles is the Goliath. The Goliath beetle is the heaviest insect and is an impressive 5 inches (13 cm) long. With its large Y-shaped horn, it might look scary, but it's usually harmless— except to other male Goliaths.

ALONG CAME

S piders, like insects, are members of the arthropod group and generally like to scuttle around. All spiders have eight spindly legs, a pair of razor-sharp fangs, and spinnerets for spinning spectacular silky webs!

Silk spinners

Other insects can make silk, too, but spiders are the champion spinners. A spider produces silk from spinnerets on its underbelly. It uses the silk to build webs, to carry egg sacs, to trap prey and wrap it up, or as an escape route to swing from! A spider can even recycle its own silk—by eating it!

Spider SILK is incredibly strong—a tiny thread is tougher and stronger than the same amount of steel cable!

Big and hairy ▶

The greenbottle blue tarantula is only a medium-sized tarantula, growing up to 5 inches (12.5 cm) in length, but it is one of the most colorful. It lives in the rain forests of Venezuela in South America and has a reputation for being a jittery, superspeedy crawler.

A SPIDER

Eyes forward ▶

Instead of having compound eyes, like insects do, most spiders have four pairs of eyes. Even with multiple eyes, however, a spider's vision is not very good. It usually senses prey through the vibrations it feels when an insect gets caught in its web. The spider then uses its fangs to inject venom into the victim.

WHAT ARE

We see insects all around us every single day, but did you know there are millions of other critters out there that you can see properly only under a microscope? They hang out in your clothes, live on your furniture, and crawl all over you!

The first person to look at microbugs was the Dutchman Antonie van Leeuwenhoek in the 1670s. He also invented one of the first MICROSCOPES.

Mighty mite ▶

The biggest group of microscopic animals is made up of mites—there are 30,000 different species, and most of them are less than 1 millimeter in length. Mites are arthropods and are closely related to spiders and ticks. They can live anywhere—from hot deserts to the freezing poles, from mountaintops to the ocean floor.

MICROBUGS?

◀ Nematodes

Nematodes are a bit like worms. Most of them are the same size as mites, although one nematode grew to 26 feet (8 m) in length while living inside a whale! Scientists aren't sure how many different sorts of nematodes there are, and they believe that there are lots of varieties waiting to be discovered.

Six plus two? ▶

This little ball is called the red velvet mite. It is covered in fine hairs, which make it look almost velvety. This tiny mite is found in most gardens and does a great job breaking down dead plants. Mites have a cool trick, too—most are born with six legs and then grow another two, so they have eight legs by the time they are fully grown!

TINY TENANTS

In the past, houses had microscopic lodgers looking for somewhere warm to live. Today, homes are much cleaner, so there aren't as many uninvited bugs as before. But no matter how clean your house is, there will always be critters lurking somewhere.

The FIREBRAT is a bug that likes to live in the kitchen, near the oven. Its favorite snack is oven-baked bread!

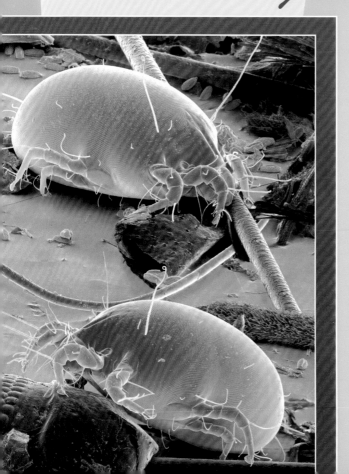

◄ Bed buddy

It's time to take an up-close look at the house dust mite. Would you like to curl up in bed with this at night? Too late, it's already there! That's because beds are full of tiny flakes of dead skin— the house dust mite's favorite food. Beds are such good sources of food that one mattress can be home to tens of thousands of these little bugs.

Share a snack? ▶

Not only do you share your bed with house dust mites, you share your food with food mites! They are very pale in color and less than half a millimeter in length, so they are hard to spot. If you had a microscope at home, you'd find them on cheese and in flour, sugar, and cereals!

Vampire bug ▼

House dust mites are not the only things that make your bed their home. Another mattress-loving monster is the bed bug. This flat-bodied, reddish brown creature loves to feed on human blood at night.

PERSONAL

With so many tiny bugs and mites out there, it's not surprising that some of them call humans home. For many microbugs, your body is the perfect place to settle down and raise a family!

Clean or dirty? ▶

You might think that head lice like dirty scalps, but the opposite is true! They prefer a head that's covered with nice clean hair.

▼ Itchy and scratchy

The head louse can't jump or hop, so it spends its whole life living on human scalps. Its saliva irritates the skin, making the head itch. If lice are allowed to stay, they leave lots of eggs attached to the hair.

PARASITE

Eye spy ▶

Believe it or not, there's a mite that lives on your eyelashes! It's called the follicle mite, because it lives in follicles, the pits in your skin where the roots of your hairs are. Even though these mites are close to your eyes, you'll have trouble seeing them—they're less than half a millimeter long!

◀ Air ambush

Little mites can sometimes cause big problems. Chiggers are six-legged microbugs that grow up to be mites. They can't fly, but they can climb up tall grass and weeds. Then they spring onto passing animals or people and bite!

MICROBUGS

Most animals are affected by fleas, and even other insects suffer as a result of unwanted freeloaders. Fleas and microbugs that live on animals are always in search of a host and a constant supply of food.

Hop to it ▶

The flea is a parasite that loves to bug your pets! Under a powerful microscope, this bug looks like a well-armored alien. A flea starts life by hatching from an egg into a tiny maggotlike creature. It spins a cocoon for itself, then waits. When it senses vibrations or moisture, it pops out of the cocoon, knowing a host is near. Then it leaps onto a passing animal and starts munching.

DO LUNCH

Bee mite ▼

Even insects as small as bees have microbugs living on them—and some cause a lot of trouble. The varroa mite is like a miniature crab that sucks the blood of adult bees. It also lays its eggs in hives, and when they hatch, the offspring start to feed on the bee larvae.

The PLAGUE is a disease which can be spread to people and other animals by RAT FLEAS that are infected with the disease.

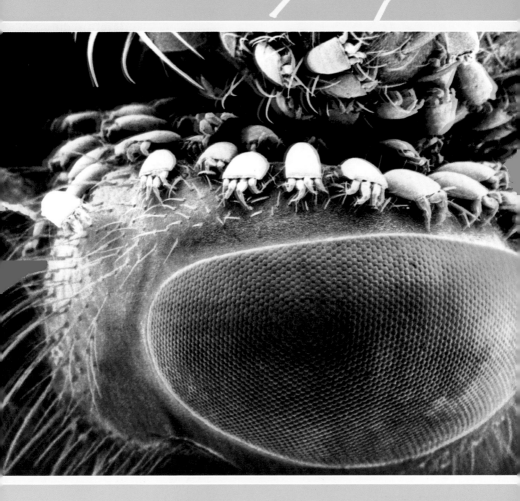

THE ROOT OF

Your house has mites, and you and your pets are crawling with them, too. So you can imagine how bad the situation is in the garden! These microbugs are causing all sorts of problems out there.

▼ A mitey problem

Gardeners hate red spider mites because these pests can turn up in both the garden and the greenhouse—and they like to eat the same things that we do! They will eat almost any plants we grow for food. Among their favorites are peas and strawberries!

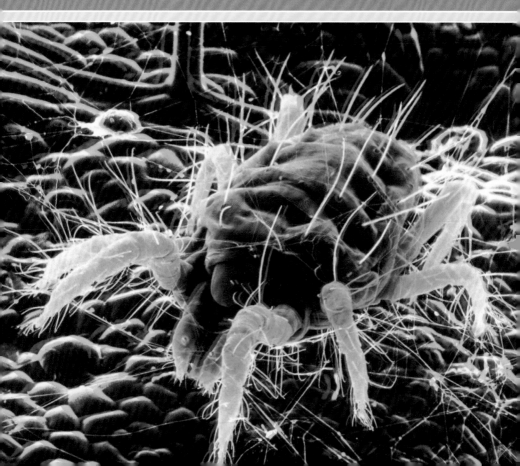

THE PROBLEM

◀ Eats shoots and leaves

Although some nematodes live in the soil, others can find their way inside plant leaves, which makes the plant lose color and die. Other nematodes attack the roots of plants and can trick a plant into growing the bits that the nematodes like to eat.

Galling ▶

Have you ever seen plants with odd-looking lumps that don't seem to belong? These bumpy lumps are called galls, and bugs are the main reason they're there. Some galls are formed by mites feeding. Others appear on roots as a result of hungry nematodes eating away.

TINY TERRORS

Although some lice and ticks are so small you need a microscope to see them, the tiniest creatures in the microbug world are microbes. There are many types of microbe, but the main groups are algae, archaea, bacteria, fungi, protozoa, and viruses.

▼ Movers and shakers

Protozoa are microbes on the move. Some are like tadpoles, moving around by beating a long, thin tail. Others have hairlike parts sticking out all over their bodies, which they move to shuffle themselves along. Protozoa move around to try to find food—including other microbes, like bacteria.

◀ Dead or alive?

Viruses are microbes, although scientists are not sure whether they are living or not! Most of the time, viruses—like the flu virus—just float around in the air. When they come into contact with a person, plant, or animal, they reproduce and make the unlucky host sick.

Bacteria ▶

Bacteria are the smallest living creatures, and they live in water, in soil, on animals, and on people. Bacteria come in all sorts of shapes and sizes, and they can survive in the harshest conditions on Earth. Almost all living things need sunlight, but bacteria can manage without it.

◀ Fungi

There are around 80,000 known species in the fungi group. A mushroom is a fungus, but some of its relatives are much smaller than it is. Two of the most common are mold and the yeast that you use to bake bread.

THRILLER FACTS

Now that you've crawled with the creeps of the bug world, you may think you know it all, but here are a few more facts that will make you a real bug expert!

Even TERMITES get bugged now and then! Miniscule microbes live in termites' stomachs, helping them digest the wood they eat.

▲ Dinner for one

The female praying mantis is a bug with a mean streak. As soon as she has mated with a male, she eats him!

Snuggle bugs ▶

There are up to 5,000 species of ladybug, and most of them curl up and sleep through the winter. They don't hibernate alone, though—they settle down and snore in groups that can contain thousands!

Two-spined spider ▶

The two-spined spider is one of the most beautiful types of spider. It is brightly colored, with two hornlike white spines. This tiny bug from Australia can change color, too!

Gut feeling ▼

Remember the microbes? They can be really useful! Bacteria help us digest our food. There are a ton of them—about 10 trillion in every human stomach.

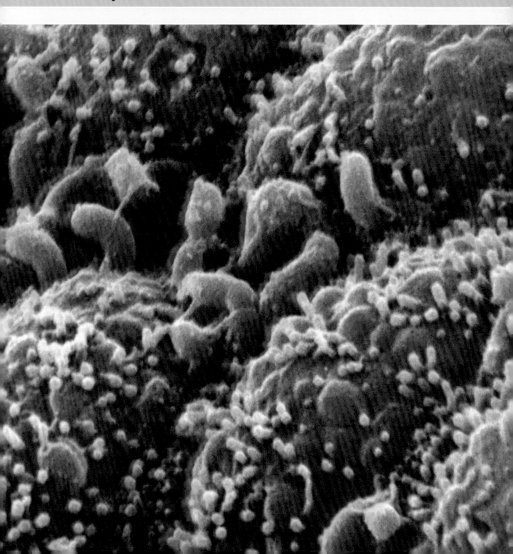

This edition created in 2011 by
Arcturus Publishing Limited, 26/27 Bickels Yard,
151–153 Bermondsey Street, London SE1 3HA

ISBN 978-0-545-28178-2

10 9 8 7 6 5 4 3 2 1   11 12 13 14 15

Printed in Malaysia 106

First Scholastic edition, September 2011

ARCTURUS CREDITS
Author: Paul Harrison
Editor: Jacqueline McCann
Designer: Tania Rösler
Illustrator (glasses): Ian Thompson

PICTURE CREDITS
Corbis: front cover
Nature Picture Library: title page, p. 3 left and
  right, p. 4, p. 5 top, p. 6 top, p. 7, p. 9 top,
  p. 10 left and right, p. 13 top and bottom,
  p. 14 bottom, p. 15 bottom, pp. 16–17,
  p. 30 top and bottom
NHPA: pp. 2–3, p. 5 bottom, p. 6 bottom,
  p. 8, p. 9 bottom, p. 12, p. 13
  middle, back cover left
Oxford Scientific (OSF)/Photolibrary: p. 11 top

Reuters: p. 11 bottom
Science Photo Library: p. 14 top, p. 18,
  p. 19 top and bottom, p. 20, p. 21 top and
  bottom, p. 22 bottom, p. 23 top and bottom,
  p. 24, p. 25, p. 26, p. 27 top and bottom,
  p. 28, p. 29 top, middle, and bottom, p. 31
  bottom, back cover right
Shutterstock: p. 15 top, p. 17 top, p. 22 top,
  p. 31 top

3-D images produced by Pinsharp